The Ol' Dog and Duck

The Ol' Dog and Duck

Mike Hanmer Walker

To order additional copies of this book, contact:
Xlibris LLC
1-888-795-4274
www.Xlibris.com
Orders@Xlibris.com
540997

CONTENTS

WHAT MY SISTER DID

What my sister did
It all began when I was a young boy, and I never

knew better I suppose

as my sister convinced me it would be beneficial to

stick cherry pips up my nose,

Always the prankster, she realised from then that i

could be easy game,

And even as I grew older and wiser, she still felt just

the same,

One time I can recall, one afternoon I was washing

my hair in the sink,

she already had this plan all worked out, well that is

what I think,

I was bent over this sink rinsing my hair, unaware

she had me in a trap,

she made me jump by bursting a balloon behind me

and hitting my head on the tap,

another time after a heavy night out with the lads

i returned home a little worse for wear,

and I should have known when I saw her grin, that

she was planning something there,

but I just went to my room and hit the sack to rest

my dizzy head,

then I felt something that made me scream, there

was a frozen chicken in my bed,

what was it doing there? who put it there? and most

of all what for?

then of course I heard my sisters silly giggles just

outside my door,

so you may ask do I still love my sister, after all she

had put me through?

well I got my own back just a few times. And yes of

course I do

POETS SYNDROME

I am in a spot of bother here, please allow me to
tell you why,

when I am thinking poetry, I can't stop rhyming no
matter how I try

is there such a condition that exists, like a poetry
disease,

if there is I think I have got it, so can somebody help
me please?

don't get me wrong, I like to write poetry and I am
happy to let it rhyme

but when I am out and about its so annoying when
you do it all the time,

so I am looking for a cure, before my condition gets
any worse,

I have sent for some help to control it, and stop me

talking in verse,

ah someone has wrote to me and said they have the

answer to my plight,

that's great I said please do explain, and let's just

hope you are right,

i was then told to end a my sentence with a word

that cant rhyme like purple,

so I gave that a try, well I have nothing to lose and i

may as well..e-r..I may as..... yeah it worked

A LAZY DAY

A lazy day
As I was sitting by my window with a cup of coffee, i

looked up to the sky,

I noticed that the day was about to break as the stars were

saying goodbye,

The first rays of the sun then painted the fields with a

golden hue,

they reminded me of what we take for granted, it is such a

beautiful view.

The birds were singing and shouting waking up the

neighbourhood,

I often wonder if they are trying to talk to us, and want to
be understood.
Maybe to tell us of our destructive ways, and what we
need to do,
to stop ruining the environment, because it is there planet
too,
Then as I stretch and wipe the sleep out of my eyes and
finish yawning,
I feel grateful as I look and realise, I have been granted
another morning.
I want to put all my troubles and concerns on a high shelf
for now, and I will tell you why,
I want to be granted many more mornings, but today just
sit and watch this one go by
Mike walker

THE OL DOG AND DUCK

I was walking down the street the other day when I
saw someone I used to know,

from where I could not remember his name and I

wanted to say hello

and then it suddenly dawned on me, yes I am sure

that is him,

I have not seen him in such a long time, but I

remembered my ol mate Jim,

"hello Jim" I said to him what are you doing down

here

there's a pub just up the road there, come and have

a beer,

so we walked up the road, Jim and I, and into the

ol dog and duck,

there was a young good looking barmaid there so

Jim thought he would try his luck,

"Hello luv you must be in my heart cos I find you so

loveable,

"And you must be in my bowel then" she replied

"cos I just find you irritable~·

"Ahh well Jim your out of luck" I said "I don't think

she wants to know.

let me show you how it's done ok, watch while i

have a go,

"Hello darling' where have you been all my life" i

thought I would give that line a try,

"well I wasn't around for at least half of it" came

back her sharp reply,

so that stopped me in my tracks, there was no

more of my chat,

i did try to think of something to say, but there was

no answer to that,

with our ego's slightly bashed, Jim asked if I wanted

another beer,

No thanks Jim I said to him, let's just get out of

here,

so we went outside and Jim said to me "I feel such a

sad ol loser"

same time next week then Jim? I asked, Jim said

yeah why not? let's try another boozer.

MY COUSIN WAYNE

My cousin Wayne likes to play football on a Thursday just

to keep himself fit,

which is all very much to his credit, as he is now getting on

a bit'

most people or footballers of his age would want to just

call it a day,

but Wayne feels fit enough to carry on, and he is always

ready to play.

he may have slowed down a little, and the tackles may go

over the top,

but even if he breaks the odd leg or two. nothing is going

to make him stop

so good luck to him it's great to enjoy your football as you

are getting older.

just a word of warning though Wayne, don't bite any ones

shoulder,

MY COUSIN ROBERT

My cousin robert {just like Wayne) likes to play football

although he is getting on,

so maybe it's just me who thinks that his footballing days

are long gone.

well we could always form a team, but I don't know how

you will rate us,

because you are both still middle aged, whereas I am

entering pension status,

but I am not finished yet, I still have the energy plus the

spirit and soul,

so go ahead and pick me, I can play but please let me go

in goal,

i think you would be glad you did as nothing would get past us,

there would be a taxi and an ice cream van too. I would not only park the bus,

on second thoughts I don't think my football career really has much of a future,

so if I do fancy playing the beautiful game, I will stick to my computer.

Mike Walker

HEALTH AND SAFETY IDEAS

Did I hear right that kids at school should wear safety goggles when playing conkers,

well health and safety has its place but I think this is completely bonkers,

there are many warnings everywhere some are of course well known,

so I have decided to help everyone out with a few of my own,

beware when growing roses, do not grab the thorns, and do not play leapfrog with any unicorns,

bleach is dangerous when drunk, and I really must admit,

so is one of my neighbours when I come to think of it.

when you argue with the missus please be sure to advise her,

never to be tempted to hit you on the head with a steak tenderiser,

and when you buy peanut butter it warns you on the jar you get this item contains nuts, just in case you would forget,

and if a soldier is diffusing a bomb and you see him run away,

just try and keep up with him that's all that I can say,

well I hope I did my bit and I done you all a favour,

and I hope my contribution has made your life much safer.

HELP IT'S HAPPENED

Help I think it's happened I have finally gone round the twist,

without the use of any substance, and I am not even pissed,

I don't use illegal substances, so it's definitely not drug abuse.

I sometimes wish it was, then at least I would then have an excuse.

so what is the cause of this? and could there be any way of knowing?

because at this very moment I can't tell whether I am coming or going,

I am now talking to the fairies, and I will be staring at the moon

I have this very strong feeling they will be coming to get

me soon

so I think I will try the old tested method, it has worked for

me so far

and that is if you don't know if you are coming or going,

then just stay where you are,

WHAT WE HAVE

We don't have any palaces, no knights or dames,
and we are not as rich as royalty

but we do have a sense of fun, care for one another, and
lots of loyalty.

we are all living in different places from each other but no
matter how far apart

we are always close together and close to each other, I feel
it in my heart,

and if any of us has a problem, and others could be there
to help you out

then someone would be there to share and help of that
there is no doubt

we give each other encouragement where needed and
plenty of support

there is so much to be thankful for and I have given it some
thought

so many of us everywhere and I don't know where I should
start,

to thank the whole of the Hanmer family for which I am so
proud to be a part

IT'S KYLIE AGAIN

I was just sitting on my bed enjoying a sandwich/

sometimes I like a midnight snack/

then I suddenly heard a noise somewhere/

it seemed to come from behind my back/

i did not have a clue what it was but I knew it was getting

late/

so I put my sandwich down and went to investigate

at first I just looked under my bed to see if anything was

there/

but there was only an empty teacup/ and some old

underwear.

then I went to the wardrobe/

and as I opened the door/

what a shock I got/ you'll never believe what I saw.

Kylie what are you doing there ? I could not believe my
eyes.

well I never expected you to be in there/

what a nice surprise

so I just looked at kylie for a while/

and then sat back on my bed/

and when kylie sat beside me, not a word was said

but then she suddenly but gently bit my fingers to show

she was in a playful mood,

I wasn't really that interested though I just wanted to get

back to my food

I knew she was getting to like mel when she gave me her

paw to hold.

my puppy dog called kylie, is only twelve weeks old.

NOT TOO HONEST

Too much honesty can be hard to take, and if you really cared.

There's a way of letting people know and their feelings will still be spared.

So come on chaps if she asks does my bum look big in these, and it seems to be a fact,

That indeed her bum looks enormous in those, just use a little tact.

Just saying I think they may be the wrong size for you, sounds so much better then,

You look like you were poured into those leggings, and just forgot to say when.

Ladies just say you have had enough for now, when he is passionate in the sack,

There's no need to bruise his ego and show your bored by putting the ashtray on his back

You only have to be a little bit honest with some people, as you don't want to start a fight,

Whereas if you were totally truthful, there's just a chance that you might,

I am not suggesting that you tell lies in any situation, but I hope that you can see,

For a peaceful life, you can get by with just a little honesty.

HELPFUL SURPRISE

Has anyone ever tried to help you out without you knowing so that it would be a nice surprise,

well I remember that happening to me once and I could not believe my eyes,

my niece Risa who was young at the time and one or two of her friends, decided to clean my car,

I was not around at the time of the event but I don't think I was very far,

when I went to my car you should imagine what a lovely surprise I had

it was lovely and clean and they did a good job, but they cleaned it with a scouring pad,

At first I thought this wasn't happening and it was just a horrible dream, but when I realised how real it was, I tried not to react

although I wanted to scream,

so I just said apart from the scouring pad you did a good job, and I have to thank you girls,

because now my car looks very interesting with lots of interesting swirls,

oh and if you wanted to do me a favour ever again, please let me know before

and then I can make a little suggestion, because I don't like surprises anymore.

OH LUCKY DAY

I never did believe in good luck that could be lasting all day long

until one particular run of events were surprisingly proving me wrong

now the chances of this happening you would agree are quite remote

I bent down to tie my shoe lace, and saw my foot on a £20 note,

and then on that very same day a similar thing happened I can't remember when,

I trod in some chewing gum along the street which picked up another 10.

but it was in the cricket park that I knew this was going to be my lucky day.

a well struck cricket ball was going to hit me, when my mates head got in the way

so I then decided on this lucky day not to waste any more time,

I went home straight away and picked 6 numbers between 1 and 49

and yes I bought the ticket that day and this may seem a bit absurd

guess how much I had won on it.... not a dickie bird

TROUBLED STREET

We all have those times when you feel alone and troubled... maybe a little scared too

well I have been down that dark and wet road. and never knew what to do

it was such a very lonely place when you believe no one is there on that street,

and yet there are others in that same situation which you never get to meet

but now when I go down that way again, there will be others I will find

someone for some reason who has a troubled mind

and they have problems and loneliness too and they are looking for a way

and yet if we ever cross paths on that street we would often
have nothing to say

so we just continue walking lonely in that street and in
the rain

until we meet again and begin to talk and share each other's
pain,

and by talking you seem to help each other, you're not
alone its fine

and maybe on that rainy street the sun will begin to shine

WHEN YOU CAN'T BE THERE

When somebody you care for needs you, and your too far away,

there is so much you can do to help, with what you have to say

it's also good to listen to them so that they know you really care

words and ears can be so helpful, for the times you can't be there

you can still let them know your love, understanding and dedication

as we are gifted in this age, with many forms of communication.

just to let them know you will see them soon, and that you won't forget.

words can be so helpful, when your arms can't be there yet.

HOW MUCH

How much do I love you? you may just want to know,
so I will do my best to work it out,

what would I give up? and what would I do for you? what
can I do without?

a chicken supreme meal, a bottle of champagne, I could
give both of them a miss,

yeah I would happily turn both of those away for just one
little kiss,

i love you more than a roller coaster ride, or even a cup
final ticket.

and I would give you the walnut of my walnut whip and I
wouldn't even lick it,

so I have worked it out on paper now just how much that
I love you,

and its all the world, 3 walnut whips and £1.32.

POLKA THE POLAR BEAR?

Polka lived with his mum and dad in the Antarctic, but he never liked living there.

in fact as he grew older it played on his mind that he wasn't a polar bear

so to try and convince him, his father took polka out hunting for the day.

trekking across the snow, and swimming through icy cold waters, he showed him the polar bear way,

but this way did not convince polka and he had to think of another.

and there was only one way to find out for sure, he would simply ask his mother.

"Mum" he asked "is there a chance I am not a polar bear?, I really need to know,

"Well of course you are" said his mum "your my polar bear you silly ol so and so"

But this did not convince polka in any way, in fact his doubts were increasing.

"I can't be a polar bear" he suddenly cried out "because I am absolutely freezing....

REGRETS

Sometimes when I am thinking of you, regrets just grow and grow,

so much I wanted to show you, so much I would want you to know,

and these regrets and questions are filed somewhere on my brain,

and often when I think of you they seem to just open up again,

Every challenge that I face large or small or even every little move,

I wonder what your opinion would be, and just how would you approve,

Would this be wrong ? would that be right? and then suddenly it all would fit,

you would tell me to pull myself together, like I would be telling myself, and just get on with it.

FREEZE A JOLLY GOOD FELLOW

What is this new craze that is catching on where you nominate someone you know.

by saying I have had some ice and water thrown over me

and I would like you to have a go,

now I am a coward and I would be scared of actually freezing to death!

so don't nominate me, or if you already have then please don't hold your breath.

and it is all done in the name and cause of charity, which of course is very nice,

however I would choose something that would not make me suffer. and doesn't involve ice

don't get me wrong if you want to film yourself taking part, I am more than happy to watch

but I only like two lumps of ice at a time and then only in a glass of scotch so although many like me may think it's silly and a strange way of having fun,

i am sure the charities who benefited from your actions will say "thank you and well done"

ok I may not pour ice and water over my head. as I may not find it funny,

but I want to take part somehow and help to raise some money,

so when this book is printed and to save it from gathering dust,

i promise to raffle the original manuscript for the Macmillan nurses trust,

KEEP IT UP

No matter what I write down now today about humanity, suffering and war.

in songs in poems and speeches we know it has all been said before,

Let's give peace a chance, John Lennon once called out in song,

and many of us listened, but too many never listened for too long,

With a lot of heart and passion, Martin Luther spoke out too.

a lot has been done, but not enough to make his dream come true.

Nelson Mandela had an impact too, from a powerful position,

and around the world he became the impossible, a much loved politician,

All heroes in so many ways their words and efforts today

mean just the same,

that's why we need more heroes like them, to repeat them

time and time again,

of course we will never rid the world of war, and its needless

suffering and dying,

but with the time and with the passion in our hearts there

is no harm in trying.

NOSTALGIA

Life of course is full of different memories, some are good and some are bad.

Becoming a parent, your very first kiss, may be among the best you have ever had.

Failures and bereavements are the ones you may agree that left you in a mess.

but they are all as much a part of life, and failures help you appreciate success,

Your first day at school, your best holiday, how you met your husband or wife,

there are so many different ones that make up the story of your life

I can't remember my first day at work, I can't remember my boss.

now there's a single word for "can't remember" but I forgot

what it was.

We often talk of these memories, with the rest of the family,

and yet somehow I seem to think that nostalgia ain't what

it used to be,

MY LITTLE COTTAGE

My little cottage in the country is a place i would really love to be,

a rustic charm with thatch on the roof and a sense of tranquility.

there i would sit in a cosy chair watching the flames dancing over the logs on the fire.

with both mind and body feeling totally relaxed and lifting my spirits higher.

feet up, eyes half closing, making myself as comfortable as I could be,

thinking of nothing much just listening to music from a classical cd,

maybe i would think of some plans, an mull over some good ideas,

with a mug of coffee by the side of me or perhaps a couple of beers.

the garden outside and the fields beyond form such a lovely view,

it would be nice sometimes to just sit by the window with nothing else to do.

it would be great to go home there to sit and relax, but alas it is with regret,

my little cottage is in my little dreams as I sadly don't have one yet

THE OLD MAN AT THE WINDOW

The old man sits alone at his window in his rickety old
rocking chair,

he looks up and down his street he wants to know what's
happening out there,

he sees Mrs. Hynes coming along maybe on her way to
her sister Flo,

he gives her a wave, and she waves back mouthing a polite
hello,

Lookin at his watch, he notices the postman hasn't been
here yet.

Then he takes a sip of his tea and rolls himself another
cigarette,

there are many people on their way to work and
everything seems rushed.

and the old man is happy he isn't on that bus, sweating and getting crushed,

here's the postman coming down the street, but nothing comes through his door.

Not that it worries the old man at the window. He just doesn't care anymore.

Now he starts to think of his clothes and pressing his shirt and his trousers just right.

he must have them ready when he goes down the dog and duck cos there's a rave on there tonight,

MITCH

Mitch was a monkey who lived in a zoo, in one of their big wire cages, and I got to know Mitch personally, as he had been in there for ages, he was captured in his native land long ago when he was just a child, so he never knew what it would be like for him to be living in the wild, I smuggled in for him a mobile phone, one with those headphone speakers, and he found somewhere to keep it, and hide it away from his keepers, it was great to keep in touch with Mitch and ask him about his day, for when it came to visiting time, Mitch had quite a lot to say. he spoke of one guy who stared in his cage, and Mitch did not like his shirt, and he let him know immediately by turning round and giving it a squirt another time he told me, when a crowd had gathered to watch the monkeys having tea,
I could not understand what one guy had to laugh about, he was uglier than me!

Mitch said he was happy there, but there was one place he would rather be, and that is back home in the wild of course with the rest of his family, now I was the only one who knew that Mitch could actually speak, as he said its opening time, I shall have to go, I will call again next week.

SONG LYRICS PART TWO

In my last book I was looking for answers to some song lyrics that I never understood, well I am glad to say I have found one or two answers, and it's looking good, for instance in that meatloaf song, I would not do that for love either, but given the chance and opportunity, I would do it for a fiver. oh and if ol scaramouche wants to do the fandango why should he be denied? but I am no good at that fancy dancing stuff, (yes I have already tried,

I have also changed some lyrics to well known songs in my other book. and I think I may do that again, so let me give "Last Christmas" another look.

LAST CHRISTMAS AGAIN

(with sincere apologies to George Michael)

Last Christmas you gave me this shirt, but the very next day the buttons gave way, this year because of the tears

I'll use it to clean the windows

AT THE SUPERMARKET

Browsing through my local supermarket and doing my weekly shop,

I saw a guy pick up a carton of orange juice . . . and then just suddenly stop, well I just went around him and carried on trying to take no notice at first, although I did pick a carton up myself, for the when I need to quench my thirst, but when I came back round again I found him still standing there, looking at the carton of orange juice with such a puzzled stare. again I never made much of it, and just continued on my way, and then I just looked back at him, was he planning to stay all day? others were looking at him too, all thinking there was something wrong, still staring at this orange juice, he was just standing there too long, curiosity got the better of me and I just had to take up the task,

I had to go and see him and try and find out why, I just had to ask. so I approached him carefully and asked him . . . are you ok there mate, "yes" he snapped "please don't disturb me, look it says

on this carton . . . concentrate, oh I found a nutter I then

thought to myself, what a stroke of luck, then I just checked

out with my shopping, and popped into the dog and duck.

MOTHER CHRISTMAS

Christmas is coming and it's a time for togetherness and family fun, but the preparation for the big day, isn't great for everyone, as you sit down to enjoy the dinner, think how it got to the table, and many of us will know it was down to mum wherever she was able. first there was the busy shops where she had to queue and get the stuff, and the constant worry and checking making sure she has got enough then struggling home with the heavy load she manages somehow, but there's little time for rest, as she has to prepare it now. and then there is the cooking in the kitchen in the baking heat, so here's the plan to show our thanks for what you are about to eat, when the dinner is finished and drinks are served, before you take a sup, let mum put her feet up, make her a cuppa and do the washing up.

CHRISTMAS DAY

Christmas day is here and are we all feeling happy, merry and bright, maybe not perhaps you went out and had too much to drink last night,

Nevermind you will recover after some of that turkey, brussells and stuffing, then everyone gets a gift in their Christmas cracker, but you end up with nothing. under the tree you see your present. and it's in a well wrapped box, then you rip off the paper to see what's inside, oh goody another pair of socks, someone suggests a game of charades, or going for a drink somewhere. but you just want to stay where you are and fall asleep in the chair, but first you help yourself to a to some more of that Christmas log, what's that noise there's a foul whiff in the air, but you blame it on the dog. anything good on the telly? well you just pour yourself a scotch. and let everyone else argue over the telly and what they want to watch. later on if you feel like it you may play a game or two, or phone a friend or family member to find what they're up to, and then suddenly there's that noise and foul whiff in the air again the dog runs out of the room this time he just knows he will get the blame, then at the end of the day you all relax maybe another beer, well cheers everybody, now that all over, have a happy New Year.

NYOING NYOINGS, NYIK NYIKS AND BILLY GILLYS

Ok you look at the title of this poem and you wonder what all is about, well think of the noises young babies make and perhaps you can work it out,

Still confused? well ok then I shall try my best to explain exactly what I meant. by holding the right kind of material against their face, they would voice and show their content.

first of my sisters children was Danny b, he would hold a piece of silk against his face. then while sucking his thumb and stroking the silk the nyoing nyoings and humming would take place,

Paul was next and he never needed silk, for him a woolen blanket was enough, again he would hold it against his face saying nyik nyik nyik while pulling off the fluff. and then there was Risa who did the same with her favourite material, and I know she may feel silly, when I remind her now of the time when she was content and saying billy gilly gilly,

I wasn't there with Marc and Jade so I never knew what their comfort noises were or what in fact they would do. and they never told me either so perhaps they think it's better if I never knew, and if this is a bit of an embarrassment to Danny Paul and Risa, and a bit of a surprise. well I think it's cute and I loved watching them so I am not going to apologise.

Printed in Great Britain
by Amazon